MW01636054

SHANGRILA

香格里拉

FOREIGN LANGUAGES PRESS BEIJING
外文出版社 北京

Shangrila

Yunnan Province, abbreviated as Dian, is located in southwest China. Due to its varied topography, inaccessible communication and diversified ethnic cultures, it has been renowned as a mysterious land. Yet the most mysterious part of this land is Diqing Plateau, an area in northwest Yunnan that is surrounded by snow-capped mountains. Featuring numerous deep gullies, spiking snow peaks and rolling meadows for grazing herds, it is impossible to see the smooth horizon here.

The plateau is one of the regions with most complicated landforms in China. The north-south Hengduan Mountains and Yunling Mountains halt the eastward extension of the Qinghai-Tibet Plateau here. The Meili Snow Mountain alone has 13 peaks over 6,000 meters above sea level, with the highest Kagebo Peak being 6,740 meters above sea level.

The Jinsha, Lancang and Nujiang rivers rush out from among the precipitous folded faults, forming a magnificent view. While their estuaries are about 3,000 km away from each other, the shortest crow-fly distance between the three rivers is less than 100 km in this area. Due to the cutting effect of rivers, the height difference between the snow peak and the river valleys can be as much as 5,260 meters.

The unique and varied topography results in typical physical geographical belts and rich resources of flora and fauna. Diqing also has a typical stereoscopic climate. Two glaciers extending from the Meili Snow Mountain belong to low-latitude monsoon marine modern glaciers, their tongues extending downwards to the elevation of 2,700 meters. Countless lakes dot the plateau over 3,500 meters above sea level. Mountain grasslands with an elevation of 3,000 meters are lush in spring and summer. In the Nujiang and Jinsha river valleys, the warm climate is suitable for growing paddy rice and banana. The Baimang Snow Mountain and the Haba Snow Mountain nature reserves feature vast primeval forests and intact natural eco-environment. Rare species of trees and plants, such as *taxus chinensis*, fir, tung tree, tulip and azalea, grow in the forests. The Yunnan golden monkey is a rare species that lives at the highest altitude in the world. Other precious animals in the area include lesser panda, snow panther, red fox, pheasant, golden eagle, etc.

Endowed by the nature with magnificent snow mountains and valleys, spectacular rivers, lush grasslands and enchanting lakes, this region impresses visitors as a haven of peace. For thousands of years, Tibetans living on the Diqing Plateau call this beautiful land Shangrila, meaning the "sun and moon in the heart." The harmonious relationship between mankind and the nature, the friendly social atmosphere and the picturesque landscapes are exactly like the remote, utopian land depicted by James Hilton's *Lost Horizon*. The term Shangrila not only demonstrates the Westerners' admiration of the life of the local ethnic people in China, but is also an ideal realm for people's spiritual pursuit. The best illustration of this ideal realm is the co-existence of multiple nationalities and religions, as well as the harmonious relationship between mankind and the nature.

As a result of the criss-crossing gullies and precipitous mountains, all ethnic people living on the Diqing Plateau are quite independent in their life styles and cultural customs. However, as Diqing is the juncture of Yunnan Province, Sichuan Province and Tibet Autonomous Region, it has served as an important channel for commodities circulation, as well as for the migration and exchange of different nationalities. The Tibetan, Han, Lisu, Naxi, Bai, Hui, Yi and Pumi ethnic groups have lived in the region peacefully for hundreds and thousands of years, forming a unique colorful culture that is dominated by Tibetan culture while absorbing elements of other cultures.

The forefathers of Tibetans in Diqing lived a nomadic life. Due to historical reasons, they evolved into a nationality with diversified cultural heritage. After Tibetan Buddhism was introduced in the Yuan Dynasty (1271-1368), the Buddhism became the prevailing part of the Tibetan culture. Tibetans in Diqing call themselves *Bo*. They are staunch, brave, hardworking and generous. They are good at horsemanship, singing and dancing. They like to express their admiration for heroes by using metaphors of eagle, sword, and horse. The Tibetan New Year and the fifth day of the fifth month in the Chinese lunar calendar are occasions they display their superb horsemanship and skills in singing and dancing. Their lively *xianzi* and *guozhuang* dances are infectious to everyone present. Their belief in Tibetan Buddhism penetrates every aspect of life. The numerous monasteries and shrines scattering in the mountains and on the flatlands, the Mani stone piles and flapping sutra streamers in the air are evidences of the popularity of Buddhism.

The Naxi ethnic group, originated from the ancient tribe Diqiang in north China, have lived on Diqing Plateau for many generations. They still use their ancient hieroglyph. Baidi of Zhongdian County is the birthplace of Naxi's Dongba Culture, which is best demonstrated by the grand rally on the eighth day of the second month of the Chinese lunar calendar at Baishuitai. The profundity and vitality of the Dongba Culture are attributed to the unusual wisdom of its creators and its extraordinary adaptability to the social progress. As a matter of fact, it is an embodiment of the Naxi people's confidence and compatibility.

The harmonious relations and joint development among the various ethnic groups in Diqing are closely related to the co-existence of multiple religions. The co-existence of Tibetan Buddhism, Dongba, Taoism, Confucianism, Islam and Catholicism, as well as the co-existence of different sects in Tibetan Buddhism such as Gelug, Ningma, and Gegyur, are rarely seen in other areas. Visitors to Diqing are enchanted by the various religious architectures, including the well-known Songtsanling Monastery, Dongzhuling Monastery and Dabao Monastery, the Islamic mosque, the Cizhong Catholic churches and the Ninggong Taoist Temple. The co-existence of multiple religions not only embodies the vitality of these religions, but also the fine quality of kindness and generosity of the people.

The relations between the local people with the nature are equally unforgettable for visitors from outside. For the local people, the eternity of life is achieved through the cherish of life. They have a special love for the nature. As a result, the blue sky, sunny days, dense forest, limpid rivers and lakes, and lush grasslands are eternal themes of Diqing. In Tibetan language, the term "animal" has two connotations: one is life and the other is love. The Tibetans never deliberately hurt any living creatures. They integrate themselves with the nature and try to maintain a harmonious relation with the nature because *samsara*, or transmigration, is a key concept of their belief. The Naxi people hold similar views. Their legends and customs reflect a consciousness of environmental protection. They are aware that the damage of environment means the loss of their life foundation.

For this land of peace in northwest Yunnan, Shangrila is more than a representation of snow mountains, magnificent rivers, abundant resources and colorful cultures. It conveys a concept and an ultimate ideal, that is, beauty, brightness, contentment, peace and harmony, all components of a haven of peace.

香格里拉

云南省简称滇，因为地处中国疆域的西南边缘，地形复杂，交通险阻，民族文化多样，所以被人们称为秘境，而被雪山环绕的滇西北迪庆高原地区，更是秘境中最神秘的地方。这里看不到平缓的地平线，却只见连绵不绝的深壑峡谷和对峙的雪峰、起伏的草甸牧场。这片高原是中国地形地貌最为复杂的地区之一，南北走向的横断山脉和云岭等巨大山系切断了青藏高原向东的延伸，仅梅里雪山海拔 6000 米以上的雪峰就有 13 座，最高的卡格博峰海拔 6740 米，为藏区八大神山之首。在刀削斧劈般的断层与褶皱之间，金沙江、澜沧江、怒江奔腾流过，形成蔚为壮观的“三江并流”景象。三条大江的入海口相距 3000 公里之遥，而在这里的最狭窄处，直线距离不到 100 公里。由于河谷纵切显著，这里雪峰与谷底的最大落差达 5260 米。独特复杂的山势地形使迪庆有着典型的自然地理垂直带景观和丰富多样的动植物资源，立体型气候特点明显——梅里雪山从雪峰伸展下来的两条冰川都属低纬度季风海洋性现代冰川，其冰舌甚至延伸到海拔 2700 米处；数不清的雪山冰碛湖分布在海拔 3500 米以上，而海拔 3000 米左右的高山草甸春夏季则绿草茵茵；怒江、金沙江河谷地带的温热气候甚至可以种植水稻、芭蕉；白茫雪山及哈巴雪山自然保护区内保存着大面积的原始森林和完整的自然生态环境，有多种珍稀树木和高山花卉，如红豆杉、冷杉、油桐、松茸、郁金香、杜鹃花等等，保护区内珍贵的滇金丝猴是世界上栖居海拔最高的猴类，其他珍稀动物还有小熊猫、雪豹、赤狐、锦鸡、黑麂、金雕等。

大自然赋予迪庆高原气势磅礴的雪山峡谷、惊涛裂岸的长河大江、丰茂的草原和幽深的湖泊，令身临其境的人们感到仿佛真的是来到了心目中的世外桃源。千百年来，生活在迪庆高原的藏族人民把这片美丽的土地称为“香格里拉”，意为“心中的日月”，这里人与自然默契融洽的缱绻关系，亲情和睦的社会及风光如画的自然环境，正是当年希尔顿风靡世界的小说《失去的地平线》所描绘的人们理想中的乐园。“香格里拉”名称的承传表达了西方人对中国少数民族生活状态和精神存在的一种崇敬和仰慕，它本身也成为人们不断寻觅与追求的理想境界。在迪庆，多民族共处、多宗教并存、人与自然和谐相生的自然、人文形态正是这种境界的最佳写照。

迪庆高原的特殊地形——沟壑纵横、关山难越，决定了生活在不同地区的各民族得以保持相对独立的生活方式和文化习俗，但是，它特殊的地理位置——滇、川、藏三省区结合部，又使其成为长期重要的商品流通通道和各民族往来迁徙、相互交往的大通道。藏、汉、傈僳、纳西、白、回、彝、普米等民族千百年来相融共处，形成了以藏文化为主体，兼有其他民族文化的独树一帜、色彩纷呈的多民族文化特征。迪庆的藏族先民最初处于游牧、狩猎的生活状态，由于历史原因，逐步发展为受多民族影响的多元文化聚合的民族，元代藏传佛教传入后，佛教文化遂成为藏族文化的重要方面。迪庆的藏族自称"博"，他们天性坚强刚毅、英勇勤劳、豁达开朗，长于骑射，能歌善舞，惯以英雄、雄鹰、宝剑、骏马来赞誉心目中所敬仰爱慕的人物。藏历新年和农历五月初五的赛马会等重大节日是他们一试身手、一展歌喉与舞姿的机会，热烈奔放的弦子舞、锅庄舞能感染在场的每一个人。他们诚信藏传佛教，并将它溶入了整个生活当中，山间坝上无数庙宇神殿、随处可见的玛尼石堆和飘扬在空中的经幡，就时刻传递着他们浓郁的佛教信仰与民族文化气息。纳西族是迪庆高原的世居民族，源于古代的氐羌，至今仍使用古老的象形文字，中甸的白地是纳西族东巴文化的发祥地，也是纳西族文化精神的象征，人们若能参加热闹的白水台"二月八"盛会，便能亲身体验到这点。东巴文化的博大精深和繁盛不衰展现了创造者非凡的智慧和对社会发展的充分适应力，实际上也是纳西族自信与包容能力的体现。

迪庆高原的多民族和睦共处、携手发展可以说是与多宗教并存互为因果的。藏传佛教、东巴教、道教、儒教、伊斯兰教、天主教等众教并存，以及藏传佛教中的格鲁、宁玛、噶举等派别的相容共处，这在藏区都是别无仅有的现象。你若能翻山越岭走遍高原的山山水水，就可以见到著名的藏传佛教松赞林寺、东竹林寺、大宝寺，以及伊斯兰礼拜寺、茨中天主教堂、道教庙宇灵宫庙等等风格各异的宗教建筑。多宗教并存说明的不仅仅是各宗教本身的生命力，更体现了信仰这些宗教的人们乐善、包容的品性。

迪庆高原壮美的大自然与生活在这里的各族人民和谐相生的景象同样也是令人难以忘怀的。在当地人们的观念中，生命的永恒，源于对生命的珍视、对一切有灵性东西的珍视，因此人们对最富有灵性的大自然就给予了特别的热爱。于是，蓝天、丽日、茂密的森林、清澈的河流湖泊、水草繁茂的草甸就成了这里永恒的风景和人们繁衍生息的家园。藏语"动物"这个概念中包含的两层含义一是生命，二是留恋和爱，因此藏家人从不轻易伤害任何有生命的东西，表达了他们力求溶于自然，与大自然和谐相处达到生命轮回的传统观念。纳西族东巴文化中也有这样的观念，他们世代流传的习俗、故事内容都存在着一种朴素的环保意识，认为破坏了环境，也就意味着自己的无法生存。可见，这里的人们与自然形成的高度和谐的状态，其实是有它必然的原因的。

对滇西北这片雪山为城、江河为池，物产丰厚、文化绚丽的土地来讲，"香格里拉"不再只是对它的描述，而更深地寄托着世人的一种美好向往，它实际上已经成为一种理念和至高理想，那就是美、明朗、安然、闲放、悠游、知足、宁静、和谐，没有这些，也便没有了世外桃源的全部意义。

Diqing Plateau in northwest Yunnan Province is located at the straight-cutting area of the Hengduan Mountains. The Jinsha, Lancang and Nujiang rivers flow in parallel for almost 1,000 km in the mountains, forming a magnificent view. Here is the first bend of the Yangtze River. The upper reaches of the Yangtze River is named the Jinsha River, which originates from the Qinghai-Tibet Plateau and flows southwestward until it turns northeastward here, forming a rare V-shape bend.

云南西北部的迪庆高原正处于横断山脉纵向切割地区，金沙江、澜沧江、怒江沿地势并行向南穿流近千公里，形成"三江并流"奇观。图为长江第一湾，长江上游被称为金沙江，从青藏高原奔腾而下，江水在这里由西南走向陡然折向东北，形成罕见的"V"字形大拐弯。

A gorge on the Lancang River that winds through the rolling mountains. Tibetans live on precipitous mountains lining the banks of the river. Upper: Sliding rope is still used as the a means of transportation at some gorges on the river.

澜沧江峡谷。澜沧江蜿流于连绵群山之间，两侧山体嶙峋，却散布着藏族人家。上图为澜沧江上的溜索，在无桥可通的大江两岸峡谷地段，至今仍沿用这种世代相传的古老交通工具渡江。

Upper: Path on a cliff, a common scene in Diqing. Right: The upper reaches of the Nujiang River. Water flows slowly at this section, with fertile farmland stretching on both sides.

上图是几乎在绝壁上铺就的山路,山高路险的景象在迪庆高原比比皆是。右图为怒江上游,此段江面开阔,江水清澄,江畔广布良田。

Yinfengkou Dike on the Lancang River in Weixi County.
维西澜沧江阴风口岩墙。

▷

Baimang Snow Mountain on the eastern side of the northern section of the Yunling Mountains is now a state-level nature reserve. Due to 3,380 meters of difference in elevation, there are more than 10 distinct vegetation belts from tropical to north frigid zone within a 40-km horizontal distance. Most part of the forest is in a primitive and closed state, which is home to hundreds species of rare plants and animals.

白茫雪山,位于云岭山脉北段东坡,现已被辟为国家级自然保护区,由于海拔落差达3380米,区内近40公里水平距离内,呈现出十多个由热带过渡到北寒带的植物分布带谱,大部分森林处于原始封闭状态,有珍稀动植物几百种。

Meili Snow Mountain, also known as Prince Snow Mountain, is located some 10 km west of the county seat of Deqin. With its snow-covered ridge extending for some 50 km, it has 13 peaks 6,000 meters above sea level. Kagebo Peak, the highest with an elevation of 6,740 meters, is in a beautiful shape of a pyramid. It is regarded as the first of the eight magic mountains in the Tibetan-inhabited area. Every year from late autumn to early winter, pilgrims come from afar to worship the mountain. Buddhist devotees consider it the highest honor to be able to walk a full circle around the Prince Snow Mountain.

梅里雪山，也称“太子雪山”，位于德钦县城西十多公里处，山脊终年积雪，连绵百里，海拔6000米以上的山峰有13座，称“太子十三峰”，其中最高的卡格博峰海拔6740米，呈美丽的金字塔形，为云南第一高峰，藏区八大神山之首，每年秋末冬初，都有一批批香客千里迢迢徒步前来朝拜，信奉佛教的藏民把能绕行太子雪山一周视为一生中最幸运的事。

Mingyong Glacier at the base of Kagebo Peak is a rare low-longitude, high-elevation monsoon marine modern glacier in the world. The glacier tongue extends for 8 km, from an elevation of 5,500 meters to a forest area with an elevation of 2,700 meters. Over 500 meters at the widest section, the glacier is thought to possess a magic power by the local people.

卡格博峰下的明永冰川,是世界稀有的低纬度、高海拔季风海洋性现代冰川,其冰舌从海拔 5500 米一直伸延到 2700 米的森林地带,绵延 8 公里,最宽处 500 多米,被当地人视为神物。

Miancimu, meaning "Sea Goddess" in Tibetan language, is one of the 13 peaks of Meili Snow Mountain. It resembles a slim and graceful young woman and stands far apart facing Kagebo Peak. Legends goes that Kagebo had been a general guarding the north part of the mountain and Miancimu had been his wife before they transformed into the two peaks.

梅里十三峰中的面茨姆峰,藏语意为"大海神女之峰",她线条优美,似亭亭玉立的女性,与卡格博峰遥相对望。相传卡格博是镇守此山的大将,面茨姆是他的妻子,两峰是他俩幻化而成。

Autumn on the plateau.
高原之秋,漫山层林尽染。

◁ Grasslands are beautiful with flowers in full bloom in early summer on the plateau.
高原初夏,鲜花烂漫的草甸。

Autumn is the season of harvesting *qingke* barley.
秋季是高原青稞收获的季节，青稞架随处可见。

Early winter on the plateau. ▷
高原初冬

Bell rings of cattle on the grazing land convey a serenity on the plateau.

高原牧场景色。牧场的色彩和随风飘来的串串牛铃声传递着始终如一的祥和与宁静。

Diqing Plateau becomes a sea of flowers in spring. Azalea, orchid, rough gentian, pyxie, red-spotted stonecrop, green artemisia and other Alpine plants bloom in full. Here is *saussurea involucrata* that grows 4,000 meters above sea level.

迪庆高原每到春季，便成了花的海洋，杜鹃花、兰花、龙胆、岩梅、红景天、绿绒蒿等等高山花卉竞相开放，它们生长的海拔高度与环境不尽相同，其中不乏珍奇品种。上图为生长在海拔 4000 米以上的雪莲花。

Dutch tulip is introduced and successfully bred in Diqing. Here is a precious variety of tulip named as "Night Queen."

荷兰郁金香在迪庆高原被引种培育成功，上图为郁金香中的名贵品种夜皇后。

Baimang Snow Mountain and Haba Snow Mountain nature reserves boast rich wildlife, including 99 species of beasts and 180-odd species of birds, 42 of them being rare and endangered species. Upper: Dian golden monkey. Right: Lesser panda and clouded leopard.

在迪庆白茫雪山及哈巴雪山等自然保护区内野生动物资源丰富,森林中栖息的兽类有 99 种,鸟类 180 余种,其中珍稀濒危动物有 42 种。上图为滇金丝猴。右图分别为小熊猫、云豹。

Multiple religions co-exist on Diqing Plateau and the majority of Tibetans believe in Tibetan Buddhism. Here is the Gedain Songtsanling Monastery in Zhongdian County, which is also called the Guihua Monastery. Being the largest monastery complex in Yunnan, it was built in 1659 on a mountain slope imitating the layout of the Potala Palace in Lhasa. Surrounded by an elliptical outer wall, it has two main halls and 100 chambers either for the meditation of the living Buddhas or used as monk dorms. At its heyday, this magnificent fortress building complex accommodated over 1,200 lamas. Right: Interior of a main hall, which is supported by 116 pillars. Some 1,600 people can sit chanting sutras in the hall.

迪庆高原多种宗教并存，藏传佛教为广大藏族人民所信奉。图为位于中甸县的噶丹松赞林寺。噶丹松赞林寺又称归化寺，为云南规模最大的藏传佛教寺庙群落，始建于公元 1659 年。全寺仿拉萨布达拉宫布局，依山势层叠而上，气派非凡，外围筑有椭圆形城垣，两主殿周围散布有百间活佛静室及僧舍，形成巍峨壮观的藏式碉房建筑群。兴盛时寺内喇嘛超过 1200 名。右图为大殿内景，大殿由 116 根柱子支撑，威严而华美，可容 1600 多人趺坐念经。

Exquisite bright-colored frescoes in a main hall of the Gedain Songtsanling Monastery. The theme is mainly religious while historical events are portrayed.

噶丹松赞林寺主殿内的壁画。内容以弘扬佛教教义、描述史迹典故为主，画面多由组画构成，笔法细腻，色彩鲜艳。

Monks in the Gedain Songtsanling Monastery. A monk of Tibetan Buddhism is usually called "lama." Strictly speaking, however, a lama refers to a senior monk with great learning, and an ordinary monk is called "zhaba."

噶丹松赞林寺的僧人。藏传佛教的僧人一般被统称为喇嘛，实际上喇嘛是学问高深、有资历的高级僧人，而普通出家僧人藏语称“札巴”。

The Dongzhulin Monastery

Built around 1574, it is located 105 km northwest the county seat of Zhongdian with the Yunnan-Tibet Highway passing at its back. As the largest monastery complex among the three major Gelug monasteries in Deqin County, it preserves a large amount of precious cultural relics such as Buddha statues and *tangka* paintings. It reached its prime during the reign of Emperor Kangxi (1662-1722) of the Qing Dynasty. Now it has 300-odd monks. Pictured here are a religious ceremony "dance in a trance" held in front of the main hall, and a distant view of the monastery.

东竹林寺

中甸县城西北105公里处，滇藏公路从寺后穿过。始建于1574年左右，是德钦县格鲁派三大寺中规模最大的寺院群，远望赭墙排列，褐窗密布，寺中藏有佛像、唐卡等众多珍贵文物。清康熙年间(1662—1722年)佛事最盛，现有僧人300余名。两图分别为东竹林主殿前举行的法会"跳神"；远眺东竹林寺。

Upper: The Feilai Monastery at the foot of Kagebo Peak, where pilgrims offer their sacrifices. Bottom: The Shouguo Monastery of the Gegyur sect of Tibetan Buddhism. Built in 1729, the main hall is designed with a Han architectural style but imbued with traditional Tibetan craftsmanship. The main hall and the gate to the monastery feature some 30 paintings exquisitely wrought by fine brushwork. The monastery accommodated over 130 monks in its golden days.

上为梅里雪山卡格博峰下的飞来寺,藏语“衮玛顶寺”,为朝拜神山的香客必到的煨桑之地。下为寿国寺,噶举派寺院,1729 年始建,大殿造型为汉式佛殿,融进藏式传统工艺,山门及大殿绘有工笔重彩画约 30 幅,兴盛时僧众有 130 多人。

35

Overlook of the Tibetan Council Hall from the Dagui Mountain

The Tibetan Council Hall, situated in the south of the county seat of Zhongdian, was built in 1724. Local Tibetans used to discuss official business and hold meetings and religious activities here. The Han-Tibetan integrated architecture is surrounded by a wall, with the old buildings of the town stretching outside.

从大龟山俯看藏公堂

藏公堂位于中甸县城南部,始建于 1724 年,主要是全城藏族议事、集会及宗教活动的中心,属汉藏合璧建筑,外环围墙, 四周为中甸老城建筑群。

The Bodhidharma Monastery built on a cliff. Legend goes that Bodhidharma came to China in the sixth century and traveled to the present Weixi County. He went into a cave and meditated there for 10 years before enlightenment. The monastery outside the cave was built in 1662 with five floors. During the Gedu Festival in the 11th month of the Chinese lunar calendar, worshippers throng the place. Right: Believers prostrating on their way to the Bodhidharma Monastery.

依山而建的达摩寺。传说达摩祖师 6 世纪初叶来到中国，云游至今维西县一带，见此地甚合佛心，便登山进洞，面壁 10 年成佛。洞外达摩寺建于 1662 年，庙宇贴悬崖建五层楼阁。每年夏历 11 月的“格都节”会引来各地的善男信女，场面壮观。右图为佛心虔诚的信徒向心目中的圣地磕长头前行。

37

Catholicism has faithful believers on Diqing Plateau. Every Saturday and Sunday, Lisu, Tibetan, Han and Naxi believers in Cizhong Village read *The Bible* in Tibetan language and hold Mass in the Cizhong Catholic Church by the Lancang River. Built by a French missionary in 1909, the church, together with a vineyard in front of it, is well preserved. The Western-style architecture shows obvious Tibetan and Han characteristics.

与佛教并存于迪庆高原的天主教同样拥有虔诚的教徒。这是澜沧江边的茨中天主教堂,每周六、日,附近茨中村的傈僳、藏、汉、纳西等民族的信教群众便到教堂中用藏语诵经、做弥撒。茨中教堂为法国传教士 1909 年所建,至今仍保留原貌,教堂前的葡萄园依旧飘香。教堂的建筑富有异国风格,但又明显融汇了藏、汉等中国民族建筑的艺术特色。它虽地处偏僻的高山峡谷之间,却成为东西方文化交融的历史见证。

The introduction of Islam is closely related with the trade exchanges between Diqing and the hinterland. Here are the Hui and Tibetan Moslems in the county seat of Deqin at the northern end of Yunnan. Tibetan Moslems wear Tibetan clothes but white caps. They conduct rituals strictly according to Islamic doctrine in the mosque built with a Tibetan architectural style and celebrate New Year according to the Moslem Calendar. However, they keep Tibetan customs in daily life.

伊斯兰教的传入与几百年来该地区同中原地区的贸易往来有密切关系。这是居住在云南最北端德钦县城内的回、藏族伊斯兰教徒。其中藏族教徒着藏装、戴白帽，严格按伊斯兰教规在藏式建筑的礼拜寺内做礼拜、过回历年，但其日常起居仍恪守藏族习俗。

A living Buddha's funeral

According to Tibetan Buddhism, an eminent monk is a reincarnated Buddha and thus called a living Buddha. His body is burned after death and the remains are consecrated in a pagoda to be preserved in his monastery.

活佛的葬礼场面

藏传佛教中活佛是通过"转世"而产生的高级僧人，他们圆寂后都实行火葬，骨灰放于灵塔内，安置在寺中。

Offering sacrifices to magic mountain.
一次祭奠神山的活动场面。

Autumn in the Napahai Nature Reserve

The Napahai Lake is 3,270 meters above sea level and covers 660 square km. Mountains stand by it on three sides and 10-plus rivers flow into it after zigzagging through the grasslands. In autumn, the prairie changes into a golden color and rare birds such as black-necked crane and bar-headed goose flock to the area for winter.

纳帕海秋色

纳帕海自然保护区湖泊面积 660 平方公里，海拔 3270 米，三面环山，奶子河等十余条河流弯曲流经草原注入纳帕海。秋冬来临，草原一片金黄，黑颈鹤、斑头雁等珍稀飞禽云集于这块理想的越冬栖息地，为广阔的草原平添一番诗情画意。

The dreamy Bitahai Lake

Hidden in dense forest, Bitahai is a well-known freshwater lake in western Yunnan. In Tibetan, Bita means a blanket of oak trees. With an elevation of 3,540 meters, the lake is 40 meters at the deepest and remains emerald all year round. Huge trees that cast shadows upon the lake and the hat-shaped islet in the middle of the lake form a charming landscape, which varies in four seasons. The most wondrous scene of the area is in spring when intoxicated fish floating in the lake after they eat azalea petals.

亦真亦幻的碧塔海

深山密林中的碧塔海是滇西著名的淡水湖泊之一。碧塔是藏语"栎树成毡"的意思。湖面海拔 3540 米,湖水最深处 40 米,右边海头续水,左边海尾出水,常年清澈碧绿。湖畔四周古树遮天敝日,湖心小岛形如礼帽,景色四季各异。春季,湖中鱼儿因食杜鹃花瓣而醉卧湖边,成为碧塔海最富神秘色彩的"杜鹃醉鱼"奇观。

Beautiful scenery in Xiaozhongdian, some 40 km south of the county seat of Zhongdian. It is renowned for its typical plateau grasslands.

小中甸美景。小中甸位于中甸县城南约 40 公里处，有典型的高原草甸牧场风光。

The Shudu (Grazing Land) Lake with an elevation close to 3,600 meters that is surrounded by tall firs and spruces. Rare animals such as musk deer, bear and clouded leopard live in the forest. There is a lush grazing land nearby.

碧塔海的姊妹湖属都湖。属都意为“牧场湖”,海拔近 3600 米,湖畔冷杉、云杉粗壮笔直,林间有麝、熊、云豹等珍稀动物。湖畔草甸广阔,水草丰美,湖中盛产的裂腹鱼为属都湖一绝。

The Birang Gorge, also known as the Shangrila Gorge because of its unusually beautiful scenery. The Wengshui River surges through the gorge but the water remains crystal clear all year round. With steep cliffs flanking the gorge, sunshine is only available at noon.

险峻而不失秀美的碧壤峡谷,别名香格里拉峡谷,听其名便知它景致的不凡。翁水河劈山没石奔腾在峡谷间,四季始终清澈无比,两侧岩壁陡立,正午时分方有阳光直射入峡谷内。

52

Baishuitai, meaning a blossoming flower in Naxi language, is located in Sanba Township of Zhongdian County. With an elevation of 2,380 meters, it is China's largest mesa with a cold spring containing calcium carbonate. With clear water flowing downward, the mesa looks like a still waterfall in the distance but a shiny multi-layered jade when examined closer. Baidi, where Baishuitai is located, is the birthplace of the Naxi culture and the sacred place of Dongba. It is said that two holy ancestors of the Naxi people, Dingba Shiluo and Aming Shiluo, had practiced Dongba at Baidi.

"仙人遗田"白水台。纳西语意为"逐渐长大的花",位于中甸县三坝乡境内,海拔 2380 米,是中国迄今发现的规模最大的冷泉型淡水碳酸盐泉华台地,晶莹的泉水层层下溢,远望犹如一道凝滞的瀑布,近瞧好似一块层叠美玉,在阳光下熠熠闪光。白水台所在地白地是纳西族文化的发祥地,东巴教的神圣之地,是传说中纳西族圣祖丁巴什罗和第二代圣祖阿明什罗的修行地。

Masters of the Diqing Plateau: In spite of different histories, languages, beliefs and customs, Tibetans, Naxis, Yis, Bais, Lisus and other ethnic people live peacefully together.

高原的主人——藏、纳西、彝、白、傈僳等民族。迪庆各民族各有不同的历史、语言、文字、信仰、风俗，却能和睦相处，共同创造新生活。

Tibetan garments are characterized by parallel patterns with increasingly bright colors. Adornments are usually made from gold, silver and jade.

绚丽的藏族服饰。其艺术特点是色彩纹样的递增排比，对比强烈，和谐统一，配饰多用金银、玉石等，充分显示了藏民族的性格和地域特征。

Tibetan dwellings. The most common are blockhouse and hut, usually with two floors. The wall is usually plastered white and the door and window are decorated with exquisite patterns painted in bright colors. Tents are relatively simple. The dwellings scatter on grasslands, in gorges and by rivers.

藏族民居，最多见的是碉房、木板房，大都为双层，外涂白灰，门窗装饰讲究，通常要雕出花样，着彩漆；也有帐房式的，比较简易。漂亮的藏式民居广泛分布在草坝、峡谷、江边，错落有致。

◁ **Hospitable Tibetans**
A Tibetan family entertains guests with delicious buttered tea and *zanba*, roasted *qingke* barley cakes.

温馨的藏族家庭
热情的主人会在摆设和家什都充满浓郁藏族气息的宽敞厅堂中以浓香的奶茶、糌粑招待远道而来的客人。

Tibetan wedding
Upper: The bride's family escort the bride to the bridegroom's village by horses or cars. Bottom: Seniors and distinguished guests of the bridegroom meet the bride outside the village. The wedding proceeds with songs from beginning to end.

藏族的迎亲仪式
上图为新娘家将装扮停当的新娘送出家门，用马队或汽车送到新郎家村口；下图是新郎家的长辈和贵宾在村口唱歌迎接新娘。整个迎亲仪式隆重热烈，自始至终都以歌唱和说唱的形式进行。

Naxi dwellings in Baishuitai. Both the house and furniture are built with logs. The platform on the two side of the fire pit is used as seat and bed. The family god is enshrined at one corner; the firelock hanging on the wall symbolizes that Naxi's ancestors were nomadic people from the north; the basket is especially used for offering sacrifices. Bottom: Garments and adornments of young Naxi women. The silver plate-shaped headdress and the sheepskin cape with four hooves are called "being under the canopy of the moon and the stars."

白水台纳西族民居，其房屋、内部摆设全都是由粗壮原木搭造的，屋内火塘两边的低台既是座又当铺；墙角供奉有家神，悬挂的火枪象征着祖先是北方的游牧民族，背篓是纳西族人家祭神所用。下图是白水台纳西族姑娘服饰，银质圆盘状头饰和有四足的羊皮披肩，俗称"披星戴月"。

Offering sacrifice to Mountain God. On the eighth day of the second month of the Chinese lunar calendar, tens of thousands of Naxi people come to Baishuitai, killing chickens and offering them as sacrifice to Mountain God. The festival lasts for a number of days. Bottom: Naxi Dongba pictures and wood engravings. The former are pictures and hieroglyph reflecting the ancient culture of Naxi, while the latter is used mainly as offering objects.

白水台上纳西族热闹的“二月八”祭神。每年农历二月初八，成千上万的纳西族人都要到白水台上杀鸡祭祀山神，欢度传统的民族节日，活动要延续数日。下两图分别为纳西东巴画和木牌画，前者用图画和象形文字反映了纳西族对祖先文化的记载和传播，后者主要为祭神用品。

The Yi people in Diqing call themselves "Nuosu." They mainly live in Hutiaoxia Town, Sanba Township and Luoji Township, most with an elevation between 2,500-3,000 meters.

迪庆的彝族自称"诺苏",主要分布于虎跳峡镇、三坝乡、洛吉乡等地,大多数居住在海拔 2500 至 3000 米的高寒地区。

Lisu people and their dwellings in Weixi County. A native ethnic group in Diqing, the Lisu people have their own language and are good at singing and dancing. Their major festivals include New Year celebration and the Torch Festival. Their clothes are mainly made from linen woven by themselves and characterized by bright colors and simple patterns. The ornaments are usually made from pearls and shells.

维西县傈僳族及其民居。傈僳族是迪庆的土著民族之一，他们使用傈僳文，能歌善舞。重要节日有新春“阔时节”、火把节等。其服饰多以自织麻布为材料，讲究色彩对比，简洁明快，饰品多为料珠、贝类。

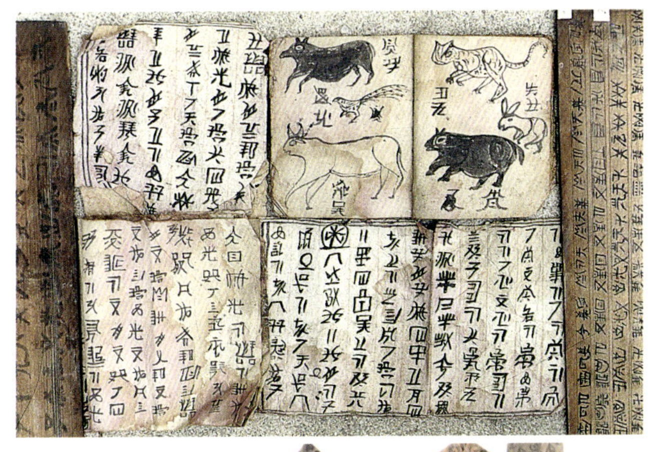

Lisu writing and wooden tablets with Lisu words. The alphabetic writing totals 918 words. The writing was created by Wang Renbo, a native Lisu, in 1929.

傈僳文和傈僳文木牌画。文字为音节文字,共918字,由维西傈僳族人汪忍波于1929年创制。

69

◁ Traditional Benzilan wooden utensils in Deqin County. The old craftsman pictured here is the third generation in his family that engages in the making of this type of wooden bowls with distinct Tibetan flavor.

德钦县奔子栏民间传统木器。居住在奔子栏的这位老艺人制作的藏式木碗极具特色，其工艺已传承了三代。

Nixi of Zhongdian County has a history of several hundred years in pottery making. Traditional techniques are still well preserved in the locality.

中甸县尼西制陶业已有数百年历史，如今这里仍保留着古老的民间手工制陶技术。

A rally of carts and mules and a caravan in procession by the Lancang River. Diqing has a 2,000-year history as a major commodities distributing center. Caravans moving north and south have left this trail on the plateau, which has also served as a channel for cultural exchanges.

澜沧江边的骡马大会和行进中的马帮。迪庆是已有2000多年历史的茶马古道上重要的商品物资集散地和途经地。南来北往的无数马帮不仅开拓出这条高原上的商旅之路，也使得茶马古道成为一条文化传播的通道，拓展了人们的视野，带来了不同民族文化的荟萃和交融。

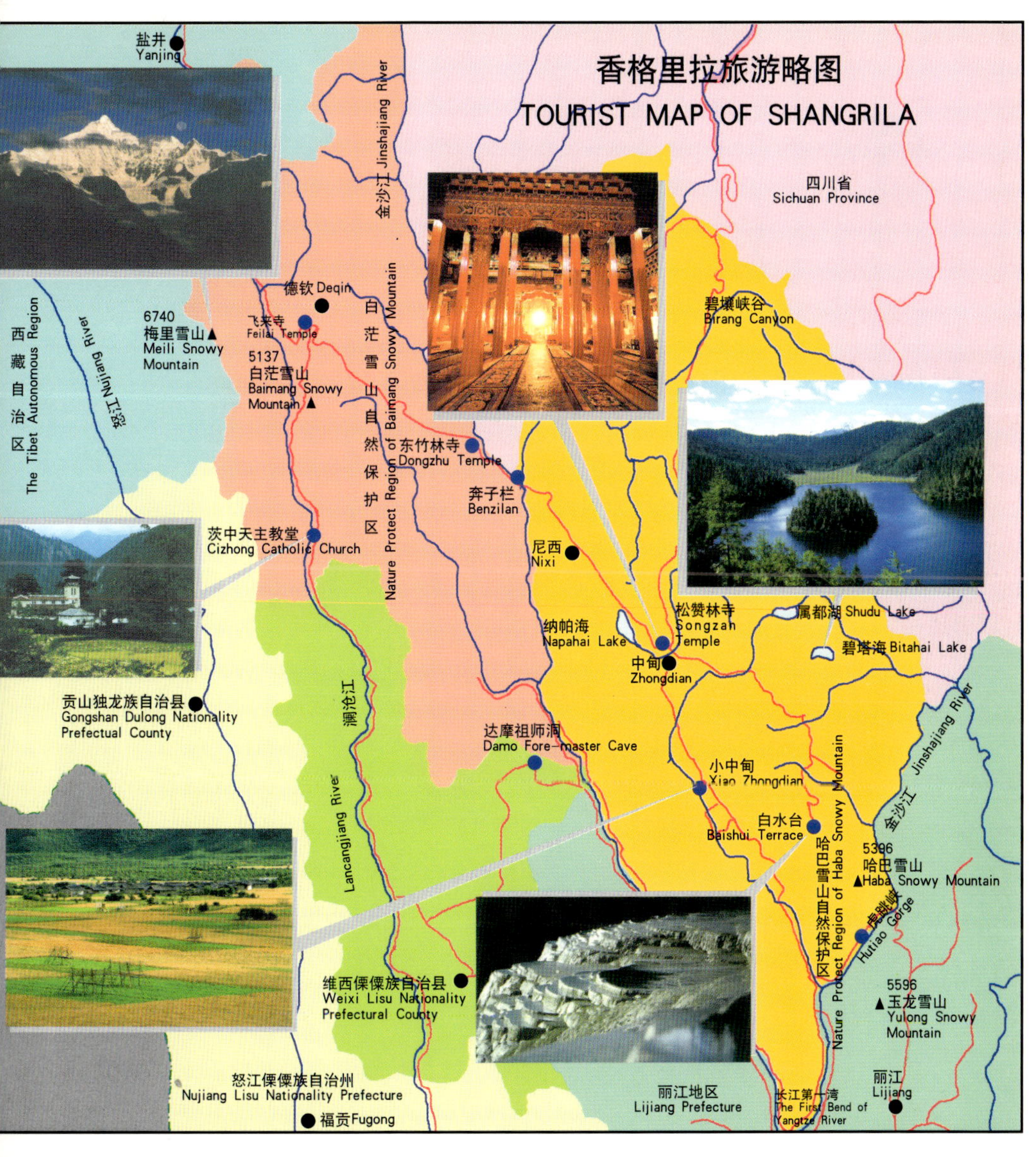
香格里拉旅游略图
TOURIST MAP OF SHANGRILA
盐井 Yanjing
金沙江 Jinshajiang River
四川省 Sichuan Province
德钦 Deqin
飞来寺 Feilai Temple
6740 梅里雪山 Meili Snowy Mountain
5137 白茫雪山 Baimang Snowy Mountain
白茫雪山自然保护区 Nature Protect Region of Baimang Snowy Mountain
西藏自治区 The Tibet Autonomous Region
怒江 Nujiang River
碧壤峡谷 Birang Canyon
东竹林寺 Dongzhu Temple
奔子栏 Benzilan
茨中天主教堂 Cizhong Catholic Church
尼西 Nixi
松赞林寺 Songzan Temple
纳帕海 Napahai Lake
属都湖 Shudu Lake
碧塔海 Bitahai Lake
中甸 Zhongdian
贡山独龙族自治县 Gongshan Dulong Nationality Prefectual County
澜沧江 Lancangjiang River
达摩祖师洞 Damo Fore-master Cave
小中甸 Xiao Zhongdian
白水台 Baishui Terrace
哈巴雪山自然保护区 Nature Protect Region of Haba Snowy Mountain
5396 哈巴雪山 Haba Snowy Mountain
金沙江 Jinshajiang River
虎跳峡 Hutiao Gorge
维西傈僳族自治县 Weixi Lisu Nationality Prefectural County
5596 玉龙雪山 Yulong Snowy Mountain
怒江傈僳族自治州 Nujiang Lisu Nationality Prefecture
福贡 Fugong
丽江地区 Lijiang Prefecture
长江第一湾 The First Bend of Yangtze River
丽江 Lijiang

图书在版编目(CIP)数据

香格里拉:英汉对照/兰佩瑾,韦爱君编;华筠文。—北京:外文出版社,1999.3
ISBN 7-119-02352-7

Ⅰ.香… Ⅱ.①兰… ②韦… ③华… Ⅲ.风光摄影-中国-现代-摄影集 Ⅳ.J426
中国版本图书馆 CIP 数据核字(1999)第 01912 号

Edited by: Lan Peijin Wei Aijun
Text by: Hua Yun
Photos by: Cheng Weidong Fang Zhendong Yang Fashun Chen Keqin Liu Jianming Zhang Jinming Zhang Wenyin He Guihua Zhu Guangrong Zhao Ting Yang Jie Li Yuebo Liu Shizhao Lan Peijin
Translated by: Deng Tianmei
Designed by: Yuan Qing

First Edition 1999

Shangrila

ISBN 7-119-02352-7

Published by Foreign Languages Press
24 Baiwanzhuang Road, Beijing 100037, China
Home Page: http://www.flp.com.cn
E-mail Addresses: info@flp.com.cn
sales@flp.com.cn
Printed in the People's Republic of China

编辑:兰佩瑾 韦爱君
撰文:华 筠
摄影:成卫东 方震东 杨发顺 陈克勤 刘建明 张金明 和桂华 张文银 祝光荣 赵 汀 杨 杰 李跃波 刘世昭 兰佩瑾
翻译:邓天梅
设计:元 青

香格里拉

兰佩瑾 韦爱君 编

外文出版社出版
(中国北京百万庄大街 24 号)
邮政编码 100037
外文出版社网页:http://www.flp.com.cn
外文出版社电子邮件地址:info@flp.com.cn
sales@flp.com.cn
天时印刷(深圳)有限公司印刷
深圳市麟德电脑设计制作有限公司电脑制版制作
1999 年(24 开)第一版
1999 年第一版第一次印刷
(英汉)
ISBN 7-119-02352-7/J・1481(外)
004800(精)